The Shining Places

The Shining Places

From the End to the Beginning

Hetty Clews

iUniverse, Inc.
Bloomington

The Shining Places
From the End to the Beginning

iUniverse books may be ordered through booksellers or by contacting:

iUniverse
1663 Liberty Drive
Bloomington, IN 47403
www.iuniverse.com
1-800-Authors (1-800-288-4677)

Because of the dynamic nature of the Internet, any web addresses or links contained in this book may have changed since publication and may no longer be valid. The views expressed in this work are solely those of the author and do not necessarily reflect the views of the publisher, and the publisher hereby disclaims any responsibility for them.

Any people depicted in stock imagery provided by Thinkstock are models, and such images are being used for illustrative purposes only.

Certain stock imagery © Thinkstock.

ISBN: 978-1-4620-0074-6 (sc)
ISBN: 978-1-4620-0076-0 (hc)
ISBN: 978-1-4620-0075-3 (e)

Printed in the United States of America

iUniverse rev. date: 05/31/2011

Acknowledgments

There are several writings now in the public domain that are alluded to or cited in the following text. Chief among these are the author of St. Luke's gospel; A. E. Housman, *A Shropshire Lad,* Poem #40 (London: Kegan Paul, Trench, Trübner, & Co., 1896); and the poet T. S. Eliot, whose collected works are to be found in *The Complete Poems and Plays 1909–1950* (New York: Harcourt Brace & World Inc., 1934).

The writer also acknowledges her indebtedness to many well-known songs and ditties from oral tradition and the music hall.

My eldest grandchild, Sarah Wilson, compiled an earlier edition of this memoir for my eightieth birthday. I therefore dedicate this version to her and to the rest of my beloved family.

Into my heart an air that kills
From yon far country blows:
What are those blue remembered hills,
What spires, what farms are those?

That is the land of lost content,
I see it shining plain,
The happy highways where I went
And cannot come again.

A. E. Housman

Contents

Introduction

Blue remembered hills and shining pathways belong to everyone, and revisiting them is a personal pleasure that can be shared with other curious readers whose interests are aroused by the recollections of a kindred heart. It is to those curious readers, as well as to my family, that I offer this collection of memoirs for their reflection, hoping it may please and refresh their own recollections of shining places.

Memories engender themselves in ever-incremental narratives. Yes, I did once remember sitting on a brown-tweed lap and playing with a dangling silver chain. And I remember being told it was my granddad Bagley who died when I had just turned three. Over my eighty years of subsequent life I have remembered remembering this lap and this watch chain—a rather different process. Similarly I have remembered sharing the top of my father's egg as a Sunday morning treat, and walking along the top of a wall, knowing he would carry me to the end of it when I complained that my legs were tired. So much that might be considered ephemeral has become, through a process of reiteration, part of a pattern I now discern in my remembered past. Thus memory regenerates and makes whole, showing a final design that gives ultimate meaning.

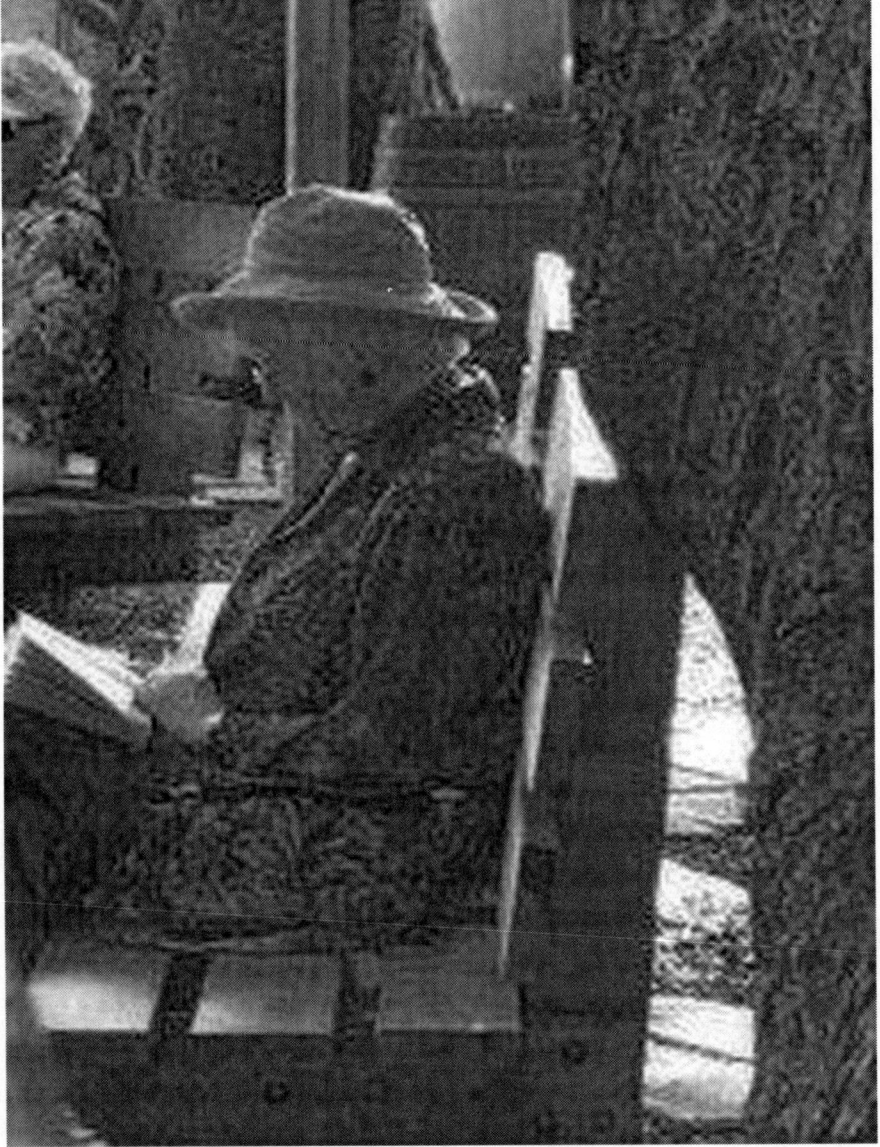

Preface

How MANY ENTRANCES does memory have? The eyes: they register images, the brain stores them, and somewhere, sometime, they can be called up again, though we can never know to what extent they then correspond to that initial impression. The ears: they make possible the rediscovery of songs from our childhood in a brain unable to store new ones. The sense of touch: skin recognizes a familiar caress, fingers stroke again the head of a beloved pet. The kindred senses of smell and taste: the nose immediately identifies lilacs and churchyards or the house where grandparents lived, the tongue remembers chestnuts and chocolate. But ultimately it is language that activates memory and makes recall possible. At least, so anthropologists tell us.

Yet which of us does not cherish some memory that is older than one's words? A memory of something important that happened before we could possibly articulate its impact? Memory is as layered as a mountain quarry where each deposit is visible. The deepest layers ensure that we do not forget to breathe, even though we do not remember much that we do remember being told we must never forget. There are memories that we have declared off-limits: wartime experiences, the pain of childbirth, the devastation of sudden loss.

There are storage chambers in the mind that resemble an old peat bog in which events have been gently cradled, and from which, like bogmen, they emerge as memories more or less intact after rocking for aeons in the marshes of oblivion.

Such emergent memories are not totally reliable. We forget the greater part of our life, yet we recall events that could never have happened exactly as we remember them, and at a deep level we know that in recall we are recreating our past. Our recollections can be the most precious way we have of lying to ourselves. Do they not speak ultimate truth about the consciousness that fostered them?

Part I

Beginnings

W<small>HERE TO BEGIN</small>? Australian Bushmen speak of the "dreamtime," postulating that in the beginning a dream was dreaming us. As I retrace my own past, the process confirms that my memories are dreams in which I am both centre and sphere—in which I am myself being dreamed. And as I sift through memories in a backward journey through remembered happenstance and recalled sensory trivia, the remembrance of things past becomes a quest for patterns and an imposing of order on what is essentially oneiric. In short, it shapes itself into one long, re-dreamed dream. Thus the facts of history become overlaid by the truth of the imagination: a truth that has always mattered more to me than any factual record. In seeking to share the content of my own dreaming with those who have come after me, I lean upon the values of the envisioned, the embroidered, the imagined.

Therefore I begin the journey with Gran, the great embroiderer.

She it was who formed the centre of my childhood world, because she was present for me in ways my mother, who toiled for long hours in the factory where my father also laboured, never seemed to be. Gran looked after me when I was too small, it is thought, to have memories at all. She lived in a three-storied old house that accommodated two of her daughters—my mother and my aunt Edith—until such a time as they were able to purchase houses of their own. A third daughter, my aunt Rose, lived next door with her large and unruly progeny, only two of whom, Jean and Edith, were girls close in age to me. These girl cousins, along with the slightly older Ondar, daughter of Aunt Edith, were like sisters to me in the preschool days of a shared dinner table in Gran's kitchen. Ondar's brother Allan, slightly younger than I, was a much-loved brother figure. Aunt Rose's sons I strenuously avoided; they were noisy and boisterous and generally odious to a pampered only daughter, and too fond of chasing her with spiders in their fists. Fortunately they appeared among the rest of us only when hungry and lived noisy lives of their own away from us, being too old and too worldly-wise to play the board games we enjoyed at the cleared kitchen table.

Ondar and Allan, however, slept in beds above my bedroom ceiling and sent me nightly messages via taps on the floor. With Jean and Edith, the three of us explored the meadows at the foot of "Gorsty Hill"— so named for the fields of gorse bloom once flourishing there—and ventured as close as we dared to the "cut" (canal) with our jam jars for bearing home minnows or frog-spawn or blackberries.

We were inseparable, Ondar and Allan and I, for the first eight years of my life. It never occurred to me to ask for a brother or sister of my own, since these companions were already there, ready to join me in any exploit. Gran cooked and cared for the three of us until Aunt Edith moved out; soon thereafter my own parents had also saved enough to put a down payment on their own semidetached home, and the first significant change in the circumstances of my life began.

Gran, however, remained a fixture. She spent her days in our otherwise empty new house, preparing my father's lunch for me to take to him at midday, cooking a "tea" for us at homecoming time, shopping and washing and cooking indefatigably for her youngest daughter, my mother. If I missed the environment of the Gorsty Hill home, it was mostly the rituals contingent upon the older house I longed for: lighting the gas globe beside the mantelpiece, bathing and dressing for bed in front of the fire, standing on the table to reach the Christmas bough suspended above it and so to nibble the dangling sugar mice, awaiting my turn on the stone stairs during family parties.

These family gatherings were outstanding examples of Gran's feats of embroidery. Once she had left Gorsty Hill and come to live with us she kept them alive in my memory by continual recounting, or by herself re-enacting, the performances of others, or by herself reproducing her own favourite song, "Burlington Bertie." She would hike up her skirts and prance through "The Blasted Oak" in the manner of the soubrette Marie Lloyd. Her own mother had enjoyed a reputation as "the Marie Lloyd of Cradley Heath," and she herself had been reared among the songs and dances of the music hall. Top hat on head, stick in hand, she had been taught to perfect the male impersonations of Hetty King. As long as she presided over the family gatherings in her own home she perpetuated these learned traditions, and all her progeny joined her in celebrating them anew.

The occasion would be Christmas, a birthday, or any other conceivable anniversary. It might also be a visit from out-of-town cousins. The precise reason for the party mattered little, because the format was always the same. Uncle Sam, Gran's sole surviving son, would sit at the piano hour after hour, playing by ear whatever a performer might require. Each performer—Mom and her six sisters, every hapless husband, and every one of my many cousins—had a party-piece that never, it seemed, was allowed to change. Uncles clasped hats to their hearts as they besought Macushla to awake from her dreaming, or declared themselves loved because they were blind. Auntie Glad, the one who was a clone for Dylan Thomas's Auntie Hannah (singing as she did like a big-bosomed thrush) warbled "Ramona." Auntie Edie, a paper poppy between her teeth, tangoed her way through "The Spaniard That Blighted My Life." Auntie Pem, alone in her disinclination to sing, donned one of Granddad's dark suits, twisted one of the starched collars the wrong way round, and visited the company as the vicar, the Rev. Mr. Peabody. My mother, astonishingly transformed into his simpering wife by an amazingly bedecked hat, stood by loyally. There was one sketch I remember particularly well that encapsulates the witty banter in which my nonsinging aunt excelled. Around the group she would go, commenting on her siblings' various behaviours, until she reached Rose, her second eldest sister and mother of those noisy boys next door. How many children did she and Uncle Les have? That I don't recall, only remembering that they were many.

"Now, Mrs. Kimberlin, and how is that family of yours? I rarely see them in Sunday school these days. I seem to remember there's a christening scheduled for next Sunday. Two o'clock. I trust you'll be there on time. You were late last year, was she not, Hepzibar? [my mother would sagely nod] and you were late the year before—in fact, you haven't been on time for a christening for years and years!"

Sitting on the stairs, we cousins would wonder at the merriment about what didn't, to us, sound funny at all. Later in the evening our turns would come, and one by one we would descend to sing or recite our memorized party-pieces. As the youngest grandchild I was last—or at least so it seems to my rogue memory, in which I was also a star.

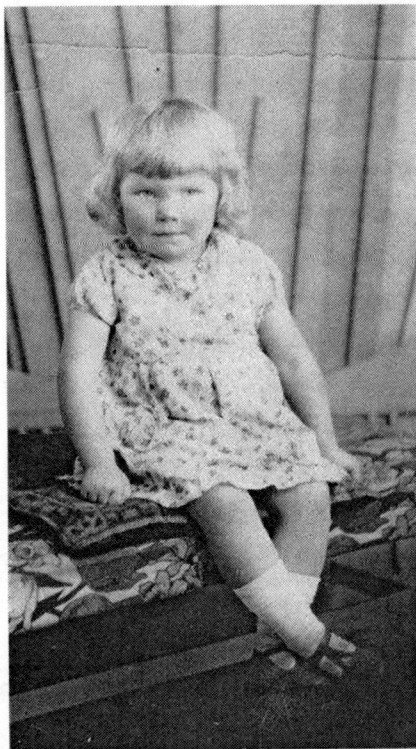

Childhood

To GRAN I was always the favoured child of her own youngest child, and she was overjoyed when I set my feet on the path leading to university by winning a scholarship to Halesowen Grammar School at the famous "Eleven Plus" examination of the time. My dear pseudosiblings Ondar and Allan also won places at a state secondary school in Oldbury, but neither of them chose to write university entrance exams—Ondar because of her wish to marry her childhood sweetheart Max, and Allan because of an intervening disaster described later. Gran, who had always told me I could be and do whatever I wished, lived on to see me well on the way to my first degree at the University of Birmingham before submitting to what I surmise must have been carcinoma. Gran spent her last few weeks in the marital bed of her own former home, now owned by Uncle Sam—the bed in which her twelve children had been born. The seven sisters took it in turn to sit through the nights beside her, which meant my mother would have been unpartnered had I not offered my company. The sisterhood agreed that would be most fitting. I was, after all, the favourite, and had reached the acceptable age of nineteen. I had always been the designated caregiver where my younger cousins were concerned; now I could repay some of Gran's caring of and for me in this special way.

Certainly I didn't mind sitting with my mother through the long watches of the night. I watched as Gran communed with her lost ones, who seemed to be gathered at the foot of her bed. I heard her conversing with her husband Harry, with her beloved sailor son Jim (lost at sea 1915), and with her sisters Alice and Millie and Sarah and Kate, all of whom seemed to be now welcoming her into some eternal communion. Being still the performer she had always been, she sang to them, "Yes, we'll gather at the river." For once the lump in my throat defeated me. I could not join in.

Our turn as vigil keepers came three times before she finally slipped away.

As I later stood beside Gran's grave I remembered those sisters to whom she had sung on her deathbed. One of them, Kate, I never knew except as a distant great-aunt who never visited us. Millie of Woodgate was a farmer's wife who sometimes brought dairy gifts to Gorsty Hill. Sarah was the one the three of us—Ondar, Al, and I—looked forward to visiting from time to time because she lived at Bournville, the Cadbury village in Edgbaston, and her upmarket home included an orchard of three fruit trees as well as tiled indoor plumbing, envied by her less well-cushioned sisters. The Cadbury family looked after the workers in their chocolate factory very well. We loved receiving the unusual bounty of misshapen chunks of "dairy milk" that Aunt Sarah, renowned for the stinginess of her larder (blue milk, would you believe!), graciously permitted us to sample. And we loved climbing the apple trees and picking other fruits from her well-endowed garden, fruits she declared much better for us than chocolate anyway.

Gran was closest to her youngest sister, Alice, who kept a greengrocer's shop in which I was allowed to polish, though not to eat, the apples. We frequently took the Midland Red bus to Leicester, via Coventry, and usually spent Christmas there when I was small. My very first boyfriend, at the age of four, was the son of the chemist (pharmacist) next door, who delighted in the name "John Fullylove," and who was later killed in the Blitz at the age of twelve.

These great-aunts of mine must have had husbands, but I recall nothing about those shadowy figures. The family seemed to be thoroughly matriarchal, and the "girls," as they called themselves, would frequently reminisce about their own mother, Annie Price, who had been one of the "belles of Quinton" and a rare performer of ribald music hall songs. It was said that her mother, my own great-great-grandmother, had been the bastard daughter of an earl, or some such titled profligate, and there were sundry other stories about blotches on the family escutcheon, which my mother's next eldest sister, my beloved Auntie Pem, would regale me with during the long winter evenings at Gran's fireside. Thus was my developing appetite for fiction nurtured by her embroidery as well as by Gran's.

Over and above all this fantasizing I can provide for the record some unembroidered data provided by my own mother, who also left a much briefer account of what she recalled about my father's family as follows: a famous "Anne Clancy from Cork," famed for both her cooking and her blarney, was the matriarch who gave birth to James Upton. He married above his station one Polly Barnsley, who had been a ladies' maid in one of the great houses of Worcestershire. She in turn produced ten children, two of whom died in infancy, before succumbing to puerperal fever at the birth of her son Walter, who was just a babe when I was born. So I never knew this grandma. Her eldest child, another Polly, took over the mothering of the others when she died, while her second eldest, my father (Wilfred Henry), became the breadwinner for the family when his father James, a builder, was killed by falling masonry.

After Wilf came Nancy, who laughably exchanged her surname "Upton" for "Downton" on her marriage to Arthur, and who produced four sons and one daughter, my dear cousin Margaret. Then came the crippled son Jim, who lived as a crusty old bachelor with my childless Auntie Polly. He bred pigeons, and I remember the loving care with which he handled them. Auntie Elsie came next. She had only one son, Brian, while her next brother George fathered three daughters. Carrie, who was a mere eight years older than I, was the youngest daughter. To her sorrow she was childless, and she is the only Upton survivor (at the age of ninety) as I write this. Walter, the baby of the family, died young. When I unfold next a scrap of paper marked "Bagley," I see at once that my mother must have had a lapse of memory, because the first name that leaps out at me is "Anne Clancy." Apparently she was actually the bride of Samuel Bagley, and therefore mother of my grandfather Harry (he of the tweedy lap), not of my grandfather James Upton, killed before I was born. Or perhaps there were indeed two formidable great-grandmas from Ireland. Certainly Celtic blood ran in my veins from somewhere, of that I am sure. In the present generation then, on the maternal side, Wilfred Henry Upton married Florence Minnie Bagley and left only me to tell the tale. But my husband, himself also an only child of the Depression years, agreed we should create a larger family ourselves. And so were born Simon Godfrey ('54), Alison Mary ('55), Margaret Elizabeth Jane ('58), and Madeleine Joan ('62)—to become hero and heroines of their own family stories—stories to begin in England before dispersion through Canada and Australia in the course of time. To these, our children, I dedicate this account of their origins and forbears.

Before beginning a description of my wartime memories I turn to a story from my childhood. It is an account given by my father of my aunt Polly's misadventure as a young woman of twenty. It appears she was put in charge of a group of even younger maidens from the Sunday school when the entire school set out on their annual Sunday school treat one summer Saturday. This day trip to a park some miles distant necessitated a thirty-minute train journey into the countryside on a little-used branch line. Polly's opposite number, a taciturn fellow named Alf, was a few years older than she, and by all accounts was a humourless chap well able to put the fear of God into his male charges. Between them they were supposed to act as chaperones to a couple dozen lads and lasses whose parents would later be meeting them on their evening return to the Old Hill railway station, so Polly and Alf were expected to be back at their respective homes by 10:00 PM. This was not to be.

Alas for British Rail. When a flurried Polly and a harassed Alf had finally ushered their mustered group into the late (and only) return train, there was a dispute about tickets with the station master, who apparently refused to permit them aboard, Polly having somehow lost her adult return pass and Alf having belligerently defended her right to accompany her charges aboard. The train bore the children away, but the two Sunday school teachers were themselves forbidden to travel until the affair was sorted—which apparently happened the following morning when Alf discovered Polly's ticket inside the band of his cloth cap.

Yes, you may well ask, as I did, how it got there.

The sequel is attested to by my father. Apparently my granddad Upton offered Alf's father a rare dust-up if the young man did not make an honest woman of Polly by marrying her forthwith. Her feelings were not consulted; indeed neither reluctant bride nor groom was considered to have any say in the matter. Unchaperoned chaperones that they were, they had spent a night in each other's company, albeit in a cheerless station waiting room, and that was that. It certainly was not a match made in heaven, despite its origins. There seemed to be little or no companionship between them, and Polly seemed to accept that her truculent Alf was the only child she would ever have. She was a loving aunt to me and to her other nephews and nieces, however, forever welcoming and generous.

As for Alf, of him I have two memories. One is more of a general impression. He was a punctilious washer of dishes, and whenever I visited their home in the evening he was to be seen swathed in an apron—either up to the elbows in suds or polishing silverware within an inch of its life, usually muttering complaints about the government of the day the while.

The second memory is quite specific. On any celebratory occasion in our own home he would be seen sitting in a corner chair throughout the evening of conviviality, morosely nursing a bottomless beer. Spasmodically he would burst into song—always the same line from the then-popular ballad, "The Greatest Mistake of My Life." Poor Alf. Poor Polly.

But back to my mother's side of the family, and my favourite cousin Al.

Of all Gran's grandchildren, Ondar was the first to pass the famous (in those days) "Eleven Plus" exam. This was the means whereby eleven-year-old children were established as eligible for further schooling at a local grammar school, thus preparing themselves for higher education. Successful candidates, who were subsidized by the state and known as "grammar grubs" by their fee-paying peers, were offered university scholarships if they stayed the course and earned high enough marks in their school-leaving certificates—a destiny I alone was to enjoy among the three of us.

But this is about Ondar's brother, and my beloved brother-substitute, Allan. Ondar set off for her chosen grammar school, Oldbury High, in September 1939. I followed by choice to a school within walking distance of my home, Halesowen Grammar School, in September 1940. Allan followed his birth sister to Oldbury in September 1941. The year Britain declared war on Germany, 1939, was a watershed year, and the future courses of many young lives were irrevocably changed thereby. By the time she was taking her school-leaving certificate at sixteen, Ondar was already in love with Max, a young Air Force cadet who was destined to fulfil his national service as an airman as soon as he could do so, and she therefore left school to pursue a career in the British Post Office. Here she stayed, cheerfully doling out stamps and chatting with customers until her postwar marriage to Max in 1951.

Allan was fifteen, and himself facing his school-cert year, when his mother noticed for the first time how he was favouring his left knee, which had a curious lump on it. It was, he told Aunt Edie, in a spot he had some time ago injured in the swimming pool at school, and which he persistently bumped each time he climbed out of the water.

By now the long trousers that British schoolboys began to wear at puberty had hidden Allan's tumour for a couple of years; the diagnosis of sarcoma was therefore made too late for the leg to be saved, so it was amputated at once.

Several times in the next few weeks Ondar and I made the long journey to the Dudley Road Hospital bearing books and grapes and family messages, many of them invented and rehearsed as we rode through the Black Country streets on the Midland Red bus, trying to match Al's own branch of humour in our fabrications. Even so he would outdo us in the outrageous comments he made, usually about the nurses—who evidently were as charmed by his insouciance as were we.

Always and inevitably he made us laugh as he did them, irrepressible and cheery as a garden gnome—which, as I told him, he much resembled. His rejoinder was to impersonate in turn all the dwarfs from Disney's *Snow White*, a movie the three of us has particularly enjoyed on one of our weekly Saturday matinee outings together. Fittingly, he was particularly good at "Dopey."

I offered to discuss reading assignments from school with him and tutor him in maths, but his answer was that he had done with school. He was obdurate. He did not intend to be a special case among his classmates, a figure of pity if not of fun. In vain I tried my best to persuade him to return and finish his school cert at least. He had decided, he said, to work as a draftsman in the Gorsty Hill offices of Stewarts and Lloyds, where our Uncle Sam also worked, and to take night-school classes to further his education as a designer. Like our uncle, he was pretty good at drawing and design, and he hoped to become an accomplished artist as well as a competent draftsman.

And so the turning in his pathway was made. Once he was equipped with an artificial leg, he became a familiar figure toiling up the hill beside Gran's house. In the course of time he became a certified and esteemed structural engineer, married a nurse, fathered three children, taught himself to play the piano. Most importantly, he became a notable painter in both watercolours and oils, and it is his still life with oranges and blue jug (after Cezanne—"a long time after, ha-ha") that has hung over my desk ever since he gave it to me as a parting gift on our emigration to Canada. Alas, despite frequent and impassioned invitations, he has never visited us here (fear of flying—ironic in one so unafraid of pain and loss), but he is always there on our visits home to England, unchanged in his humour and his empathy. My brother, my friend for life, Allan remains a constant in my life as a reminder of the courage attainable by those afflicted in unimaginable ways, and an exemplar of the triumph of the human spirit.

Ondar's wedding picture shows Allan on the extreme left of the group

WWII and University

FOR THE MOST part, my memories of the seven years (mostly wartime) I spent at Halesowen Grammar School form a blurry compendium of pleasures (on the hockey pitch and in theatrical and choral performances) and pain (academic subjects I could not shine in, such as physics and economics). There were exciting visits to Stratford, and, once I was a prefect, pleasurable exercises of power over unruly twelve-year-olds. I made my mark as a witch in the Scottish play, as Maria in *Twelfth Night,* and as Lady Teazle in *School for Scandal.* I auditioned for RADA (the Royal Academy of Dramatic Art) and wrote entrance exams for Oxford, and in both cases was advised to try again next year.

After the first few air raids during school time, which we spent in specially built Anderson shelters in the school grounds (what a frolic that was!), the warnings went unheeded. Despite local bombing hits, the school itself, like my hometown, remained relatively unscathed—just a few broken windows. When night-time air raids were at their worst we sought shelter, as did most families, first in the garden Anderson shelter and later beneath the stairs within the house, but eventually the commonly heard saying "If the bomb has my name on it, it will find me" held sway, and we thumbed our noses at the Messerschmitts overhead.

In retrospect, the war years were a time of tightened belts and highly developed patriotism. "This England never did, nor never shall/Lie at the proud foot of a conqueror." Generally speaking, the masses were better fed while rationing was in effect than they had ever been before, and we all got our daily doses of orange juice and cod liver oil.

I shamelessly accepted sweet coupons from my Upton uncles George and Jim in return for running errands; with my cousins I scoured the hedgerows for hips and haws. It was called "the war effort," and it coloured my young life much as the role of babysitter to my younger cousins did. My aunts held me to be a highly privileged only child, being educated above my station, and sought to keep me in my place by putting me in charge of weekly outings—Saturday afternoon at the movies and Sundays at Sunday school—or holiday rambles to Clent or Walton, the local beauty spots, both visible from my home (hence located on "Walton Avenue").

By the time the war ended I was in the sixth form at HGS and I remember "V-E Day" celebrations in the avenue—salmon sandwiches and jelly—as well as at the various other street parties I attended in my capacity as family nursemaid. That evening I recall being one of a long line of young people meandering arm-in-arm from Rowley Church to High Street bottom belting out "There'll always be an England ..." All was joy and thankfulness as the boys came home.

"V-J Day" was a much quieter affair, and adults I respected, such as church ministers and schoolteachers, sadly shook their heads about Hiroshima and Nagasaki. My dear father also shook his head, and bade me reconsider my former stance of "my country, right or wrong." I reflected and became a pacifist, my future antagonism toward nationalistic fervour and the glorification of war taking strong root, to flower fully at the time of Suez and to result in emigration.

But that was yet to come. At sixteen, when the war ended, I was making decisions about my future, having my sights set on university and RADA. I found myself also becoming more and more interested in theology, taking scripture knowledge as one of my principal subjects for "higher school cert," as it was then called. My newly minted worldview led to my taking up lay preaching in the local Methodist circuit as the youngest local preacher ever, and by the time I entered university I had resolved to add theology to English in my studies there. Thus it was I ended up with a double honours degree equipping me to teach English and scripture in an English grammar school. But, to mix metaphors, there were a few hiccups along this path. I first attempted to pursue my chosen goal at the University College of London in Leicester, where I had second cousins willing to put me up and where several of my school friends were also registering. Once there I found there was no extant department of theology, only an extramural course of little practical value. I therefore decided to gain a diploma in English from London University, in which I succeeded with a "first," and to apply to the University of Birmingham as a sequel. And thus it was I met my future in the shape of a medical student, as otherwise might never have happened.

I don't regret the time spent at Leicester. It taught me to value my home as only being away from it does. There was even a memorable occasion when I danced with David Attenborough, whose father was the principal of the college and who attended a student ball in company with his brother Dickie. There was also a visit of a few weeks from my French friends, Claude and Bouboule, in whose homes I had acted as "au pair" the previous summer, and with whom I was later to reconnect as a Canadian tourist.

So to Brum, and my three years in the Department of Theology, where I was the only woman in classes comprising young ordinands. What delight the OT professor took in making fun of my unlooked-for presence in his Hebrew classes.

This beaky-nosed Dr. Sparkes, who was also head of the Theology Department, was a renowned misogynist. He regularly made fun of my being accompanied to class by young clerics, and once amused them by misquoting Isaiah: "Woe to the women of Samaria, with their earrings and their tinkling ornaments, their rings and their nose-jewels and their bracelets, who walk with stretched forth necks and wanton eyes, mincing and making a tinkling with their feet"—all because I had the temerity to be wearing earrings that particular day. On another occasion he chided me for omitting a daghesh from a Hebrew word in my written exercises, and painted one on my nose as punishment. In hindsight it is not difficult to see what really ailed this scholar.

Despite his efforts to deter me, however, I stayed the course and graduated with double honours. Meanwhile I was also acting and singing in university productions, so that in my final year I met peers who have remained lifelong friends: Alec and Jean Nisbett, already married in their early twenties, Graham Beaumont and Valerie Evans, to be briefly married in their midtwenties, and Alan Clews, to become my lifelong husband. Alan speaks of first seeing me as I sat awaiting my turn at an audition. My first memory of him is of the play in which we were then cast (*The Insect Play* by the brothers Capek)—he as the ichneumon fly and I as Mrs. Cricket—in the course of which enactment he stabbed me with a rubber dagger and dragged me to his lair to feed his insatiable larva. Some beginning, particularly as his first words to me were, "Gosh, you're heavy!" He kept that dagger for years, but it didn't cross the Atlantic with us. Alec later directed Valerie and me in a play by Christopher Fry (*A Phoenix Too Frequent*), while Graham and Alan both sang chorus in the Gilbert and Sullivan productions in which I also performed: *Iolanthe*, *Trial by Jury*, and *Pinafore*.

These young men were in their final year of medicine, and Jean was secretary to the dean of medicine—she and Alec had both known Graham for years in their home town of Coventry, so that when the two medics became interested in the two actresses, the Nisbetts were happy to invite all four to parties and play-readings at their tiny apartment. So it was we had become a sixsome by the time I was writing finals.

Alan's ultimate fate had already been sealed, however, by events at the Guild Ball of my graduating year, where we six sat together at dinner and where I was much impressed by the savoir faire with which Alan ordered wine. We danced several hours away, and when he later offered me a ride home I confidently expected to be ensconced in a Bentley or a Rolls. I stood expectantly in my ball gown on the steps of the Union building, where he finally came putt-putting up on a BSA Bantam motorcycle. Ah, me. I hitched up my skirts and climbed up behind him.

This was the first of many rides we thus took together. When I graduated a month later and left home for Yorkshire, Alan was still a few months away from his finals, so he would regularly drive up to Wath-on-Dearne, where I was teaching at the local grammar school, to spend a Sunday with me at the home of the venerable old lady with whom I boarded.

Once we drove together thence through a rainstorm to a twenty-first birthday party in Wolverhampton, where another dear university friend, Daphne Russell, lived. Arrival there furnished my first memory of the restorative power of brandy.

There was no pillion on this beloved vehicle, just a square of latex, so riding behind Alan was uncomfortable at the best of times. Nevertheless during the next couple of years we frequently made the journey from my home in Blackheath to his home in Newcastle, thirty miles or so but a journey of at least an hour because it was built-up all the way. Once, memorably, we undertook a youth-hostelling vacation in the Lake District, from which we returned carrying a puppy between us to a new home in Blackheath.

Equally memorably, in 1951 we spent a summer week on the Broads with Alec and Jean as our chaperones, befriending cows as we ostensibly learned to sail. There were a few near misses as we inexpertly tacked and navigated the lochs, but all ended well. These four friends, along with Daphne, were in full force at our wedding, an event that begins both the second part of my life and of this story.

courting couple at Clent

*The Clews wedding, with Lily (Mum), Walter (Dad), Valerie, Graham, friend's
daughter Carol, Alan, Hetty, Daphne, Wilf (Pop), and Minnie (Mom)*

Marriage: An Essay

My misleading childhood reading (Austen, Dickens, Trollope) suggested marriage was a culmination—even the ultimate goal of life—the designed "happy ending." Of course this isn't true. Marriage is really a second beginning, a mutual setting out on a future in which the "I" becomes a "we"; in which to be alone is to be just the two of you; in which opinions, decisions, moods, and indeed every swing and roundabout of life are to be a shared enterprise "from this time forward" into incalculable distances of time.

Every marriage is a journey of accommodation. In a long marriage, both partners mutate; the people who set out together are not the same two people after ten years, let alone after thirty or more. When accommodation is no longer possible it is usually because one or the other has become so much someone else as to be on a different journey.

Our marriage has been like many, if not most: a river with calm reaches, treacherous bends, and episodes of white water to be navigated with caution and steady nerve. We are dissimilar temperamentally. Alan is confrontational, radical, a delighter in intellectual debate, while disarmingly loving and generous. I am more accepting and peacemaking, but given to brooding and holding grievances. He thinks; I dream. That said, we mesh entirely in tastes and inclinations, can always fire each other with new interests, and have laid down over the years that rich sediment of shared reference and mutual recognition familiar to all who have known a long companionship. After many years of marriage there is a third and shadowy presence that is an entity—the fusion of you both—who walks beside you. It is your corporate experience, a private existence, invisible to and impenetrable by others. Should it be extinguished, you are left with only the solace of having once enjoyed that mysterious and miraculous creation of shared lives.

In his beginning work as a poet, "The Waste Land," T. S. Eliot wrote:

> Who is the third who walks always beside you?
> When I count, there are only you and I together
> But when I look ahead up the white road
> There is always another one walking beside you
> Gliding wrapped in a brown mantle, hooded,
> I do not know whether a man or a woman
> But who is that on the other side of you?

He was, critics agree, descanting upon the Emmaus Road resurrection story as it is found in St. Luke's gospel, but to me the allusion is a perfect illustration of what I have tried to explain about marriage. And it is with this image of the hooded third figure that I now move from the solipsism of my own earlier memoir to the post-Alan, or post-"walking beside you," story.

It is my hope that the children who have blessed our shared lives will recognize this recorded inheritance for what it is—a legacy—and that they will value it as a means of rekindling memories for their own children to enjoy.

At the end of his life, Eliot wrote the splendid "Four Quartets," in which these memorable lines occur:

> What we call the beginning is often the end
> And to make an end is to make a beginning.
> The end is where we start from.

We shall not cease from exploration.
And the end of all our exploring
Will be to arrive where we started
And know the place for the first time.

Or, to quote a motto attributed to Mary Queen of Scots,

In our beginning is our end, and in our end is our beginning.

Part II

From Britain to Canada

I WAS TWENTY-ONE WHEN I graduated and met Alan, and twenty-three when I became half of the unit described in the preceding comment on "Marriage." We became engaged in the interim, and I was proudly showing off my engagement ring, which Alan had worked in Cadbury's chocolate factory to buy (from one of Birmingham's many antique jewellery stores), during my first year of teaching English and scripture to the sixth-formers of Wath-on-Dearne Grammar School. It was back to this school I returned following our April 1953 marriage, having a perceived obligation toward students writing their school-cert exams in June.

Our wedding, in High Street Methodist Church (where I first became a lay preacher, and to which all my local pals belonged), was attended by our university group, as well as the Clews and Upton/ Bagley family members. Graham acted as best man, and Valerie, along with Daphne, was a bridesmaid, as was little Carol Pollard, daughter of church friends. The Reverend J. Gordon Webb, my esteemed mentor in all my growing-up years, came out of his retirement to pronounce us man and wife. Alan's Uncle Tom, travelling via the city ring-road from nearby Coventry, almost didn't make it and was uncharacteristically late. My mother's sisters, along with the Ladies' Union, produced a marvellous chicken dinner in the church hall, many speeches were made and I heard not a word of them. I'm told that after we had been driven off by Uncle Jess to New Street Station for the first leg of our honeymoon, the wedding party continued into the night at 4 Walton Avenue, with my parents serving up innumerable cups of tea along with stories of my youth.

The train on which we travelled to London was called "the Honeymoon Express" because it had been specially timetabled to accommodate the hundreds of couples choosing April 4, 1953, as their wedding day. There was a simple and utterly unromantic reason for this, which had to do with the most auspicious time for the filing of income-tax returns. The result was a train was full of couples trying to find empty compartments while appearing to be much married, and the floors were awash in confetti.

Our very first airplane flight took place the next morning, when Air France whisked us over the channel to Paris. This was another unromantic journey. First we were metaphorically bumped because of overbooking, and then we were literally bumped because of bad weather, so that I needed to use a brown paper bag. Our late arrival in Paris meant that the French friend who had intended to take us to Chartres had to cancel that trip. Nicole was the "French conversation" teacher at Wath, and she was very helpful in furnishing us with a Michelin-Guide-inspired list of accommodations and restaurants. It was with her family that we enjoyed our first Parisian dinner; the rest of the week we lunched daily on picnic fare in the various parks and sought out her recommended places for the evening meal. Two of these were particularly memorable.

The first was the Bon Bock in Pigalle, where we shared a long table with all the other diners ("Le pot-au-feu—c'est pour tout le monde?" "Mais oui, Madame, certainement!"). The second was Chez la Mere Catherine in Montmartre, where a violinist played "La Vie en Rose" at our table (Alan steadily demolishing his canard a l'orange the while), before bidding the fellow dinner guests to salute us—"Vive les nouvelles mariees!"

And so to bed. This was to L'Hotel Andre Gill, in a quiet square in the heart of the Moulin Rouge district. Despite being in such a rowdy quarter, the hotel itself was quiet and seemly, with a placid chambermaid who toiled up the stairs each morning with a tray of coffee and croissants—thus beginning for me a lifelong love affair with both. On the dresser at the foot of the bed stood Alan's second gift of flowers, a bouquet of pink tulips. (His first, on my birthday the summer he proposed beneath the trees at Clent, had been a similar spray of red roses and a book of poems, Palgrave's *Golden Treasury*.)

From this retreat we sallied forth each day to explore the environs, tangling with the noisy, darting taxicabs and slowing to a saunter beneath the blooming chestnut trees of the Champs-Elysées, munching baguettes in the Bois de Boulogne, once more sallying forth in the evening for a Michelin-Guide-selected café for dinner followed by a show at one of the many theatres (up in the gods, all we could afford). Thus it was we saw *Medea, Phèdre, Black Orpheus* (Sartre's rewriting of the myth of Orpheus and Euridice), and a totally unmemorable musical called *Sous les Toits de Paris* (as well as two other even more totally forgettable offerings.) These bookings had been made executively by Nicole, so the emphasis on Greek myth, besotted women, and doomed love pairings was as much her choice as mine. Not that I noticed such propensities at the time, being somewhat preoccupied with translating for Alan as we watched. Having spent time as an au pair at seventeen, I was by now fully bilingual, and as well as admiring French culture I have always enjoyed prattling in French. Vive la différence!

As a newlywed I returned to Wath for a term and saw my students through their graduating exams. In some ways I was sad to leave West Riding, where for two years I had been welcomed and happy in my work. By the summer, however, I had accepted an inferior posting to Lozelles Secondary Modern School in industrial Birmingham, because Alan was now interning at Dudley Road Hospital and we had found a flat on the Hagley Road to call our very first own home. This was the topmost floor of an immense—to us children of semi-detached homes—Victorian structure owned by an eminent professor of philosophy at our alma mater and conveniently located on the bus route to Lozelles, where I daily toiled teaching English to indifferent young women whose sole aim was to leave school as soon as they legally could do so. At the same time I was enrolled in the graduate program in the Theology Department at the university, working toward an MA with a thesis on William Blake. Whenever possible I joined Alan in his cell at Dudley Road Hospital, where he was continually on call, and where I sometimes—against the rules—spent the night, slipping out in the very early morning. At least I did so until a sharp-eyed sister caught me and berated me about it. After that I no longer dared to share the tiny hospital bed.

Alas, the University of Birmingham classes had to be postponed when I found myself pregnant by October that same year. By Christmas my stint at Lozelles was over and so was our tenure at the Hagley Road flat. I returned to my small bedroom in my parents' home to await the arrival of our firstborn, and Alan, having completed his internship, set off for his obligatory two years of national service.

Of course this was a very happy time for "Mom and Pop," as I called my parents (Alan's parents were "Mum and Dad"). They didn't in the least mind having piles of wedding gifts and baby stuff stored in their tiny box-room, or our very first car (a baby Austin affectionately known as "Blue") parked in their narrow driveway. They were delighted when Alan was occasionally able to come for a twenty-four-hour leave, and Mom loved having me accompany her to the weekly Wednesday afternoon gatherings of all her sisters. My cousin, Auntie Rose's Jean, also became pregnant later that same year, and together we shared with our aunts all the current lore we had picked up at antenatal classes. Our first baby was due the third week of May, and since we had no car and no phone we made arrangements that I would send Alan a telegram from a phone box half a mile away to say I was "on the way" to Dudley Road Hospital (by taxi) once I found myself in the early stages of labour.

Alan had a weekend leave May 8–9 that year (1954), and we drove to one of our favourite beauty spots, Snowdon, with Mum and Dad. Alan and Lily strode off up the hillside while Dad helped me climb a gentle slope at the foot of the mountain, then we returned to Walton Avenue for tea. Once Mum and Dad had driven home to Newcastle, and Alan had driven back to Woolwich, where he was physician in a military families' hospital, I went thankfully to bed. But not for long. At 1:00 AM I realized something untoward was happening and slipped out of the house without waking Mom and Pop. By the time I got back, the waters had broken. This of course pleased Mom, who was able to fuss over me until the taxi arrived and bore me off with my little bag of tricks.

And so it was that Alan received the telegram the morning after his leave ended and had to rush back to Birmingham to welcome his son. Simon had been born with the helpful advice of four or five of Alan's recent fellow interns and the delivery room had been rather like a three-ring circus. One of his most esteemed peers, a Yugoslav named Swanco, dropped by to see me a few hours later and greeted me by saying, "Well, we have seen the shining Alan!"

The following weeks were occupied by this shining Alan in seeking a flat in Blackheath London, close to his Woolwich hospital. We eventually became happy hosts to family and friends in a top-floor (again!) apartment overlooking the famous heath of Dick Turpin fame, where I wrestled with problems of manoeuvring pram and baby and groceries up and down three flights, and whence we often made a Sunday stroll to Greenwich. So we decided to look for some alternative place of residence, and Alan found an ad in a local newspaper that seemed the answer to our prayers.

So it was that for a few months we were a happy family in a family house in Erith, where we were accommodated rent free while Alan served as a resident locum weekends and evenings for a local practitioner. This gentleman kept his own apartment there for occasional use and asked only that we maintain his property for him, which was easy enough. For a while I was a very contented resident cook and bottle-washer. The blow came when Alan, having refused a promotion that would have meant moving yet again, received an overseas posting to Malaya. Slow learners that we were, we had failed to realize you don't refuse promotions in the army. You do always as the army dictates.

Small wonder we were both alienated by these dictates, particularly when we were told that if Alan were to sign on for a further year of service, his wife and child would be able to accompany him abroad. Prefiguring Liza Doolittle, "Not bl——— likely," said I, preferring a year apart to two further years of being a rank-conscious army wife. Thus again the die was cast. If we were to have a second child before Simon was three—our plan—then we had only a small window of opportunity before Alan flew east. Alison complied readily, as she has always done, and I would be six weeks pregnant when the window closed. Back to Walton Avenue, then, and a pleased Mom and Pop. Alan's last visit there before the separation was for Simon's first birthday, and we were together able to enjoy watching our pride and joy receive his first teddy bear. By the time Alan returned a year later, this daughter would be five months old. In the interim Alan enjoyed providing antenatal and birth care for Malay women, and was even able to spend leave-time climbing Mount Kinabalu in Borneo. The telegram he sent me read "Safe—stop—unsuccessful" (a mistake for "Safe and successful," as it later turned out). My own telegram to him on Alison's safe arrival on December 12 fared better. Letters and pictures rapidly followed. Our first daughter was like a little silver-topped elf, with staring blue eyes and a button nose, and her loving disposition ensured that she would give her new daddy a boisterous welcome—as indeed she did.

We were thankful indeed that the years of military servitude were over, and now there followed a series of locums while Alan sought a place in a family practice.

By midsummer Alan had agreed to become an "assistant with view" in a busy practice in Wythenshaw, Manchester, and we had found our fourth apartment in the home of the Crosdales, who owned an antique shop in Chorlton-cum-Hardy and who were to become our very good friends. Here it was that Simon developed a penchant for wheeling his baby sister up and down outside the house, and where he once stripped the Crosdales' garden of flowers, which he then presented to me: "Mommy, for *you*!" Here we entertained not only our parents, but also other remoter family members such as Aunt Carrie and her husband Harry—who suffered through the first act of the first performance in England of Becket's *Waiting for Godot* at the Manchester Playhouse before we mercifully took them to a nearby pub until it was time to relieve our babysitter. The most momentous world-event of our married lives brought this happy period to an end. Along with other officers who had recently served in the Middle East, ominously called "Z reservists," Alan was recalled into the army for service in North Africa during the 1956 Suez crisis. Tearful farewells followed, and yet another return to take up temporary (?) residence at Walton Avenue. Pop again shook his head. So much for the "my country, right or wrong" attitude of the war years. I began a letter-writing campaign, joining many others as disenchanted as myself in deploring Britain's unjust invasion of Libya. Meanwhile, Alan's letters home—such as arrived at least—were censored. But I knew how he also protested a situation he could not change. Remembrance Day 1956 I shall always recall as a time when after days of hearing nothing I did not know whether I would ever see him again, and the hymns of the service seemed hollow and specious.

But Sir John Hare finally answered my letters. An official missive from the War Office dated December 12 (Alison's birthday!) assured me that my husband would be home for Christmas. The long ordeal seemed to be at an end. Fortunately Drs. Wyder and Wolfendale had kept Alan's assistantship open for him and now urged him to return. So this time we decided our fortune had changed to the point where we could look for a house to live in. A house of our own—what bliss that would be. I thought we could forgive Anthony Eden his folly and again accept England as our home—though Alan had returned from the scandalous war wondering whether he should not perhaps emigrate. I could not willingly assent. Perhaps if we found a home?

Accordingly Mum and Dad drove us around Cheshire looking at homes old and new. We settled on a brand new detached house in Baguley Hall. In a street full of similar homes for young professional families such as ours we chose number 25, and with the help of our parents arranged to mortgage our lives away for several years. We could afford only the bare minimum of furniture, but the house had a lovely back view to a wood flanking the Princess Parkway; backyards were strewn with toys and swing sets; young playmates for the children abounded; their parents were equally friendly. There were numerous parties (with a sound system rigged up by one of our menfolk that enabled us to listen in on respective bedrooms). I particularly remember a treasure hunt that required us to make forays hand-in-hand with a spouse not our own into the back gardens and over the rooftops looking for clues (many puns here) while neighbours on the other side of the street, mostly from an older generation, leaned on their spades and shook their heads about our playfulness. Life was very good again.

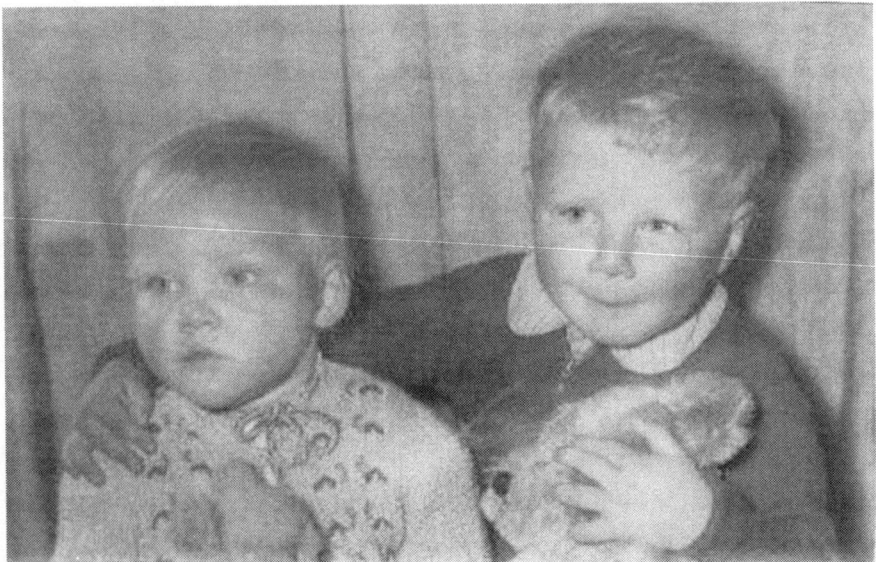

Memories of this home are happy ones. It was here that Simon painted his baby sister's trusting face with enamel left behind by builders in an upstairs cupboard, so that for weeks traces of black made tracks over her cheeks below her wispy silver hair and had to be explained to pram-peepers. Once she was toddling around the back gardens, she would struggle to our back door with arms full of neighbourhood toys: "*Mine*," she would happily declare. We joined the local Wesleyan Church and its young minister, John Vincent, became a frequent visitor, while choir practices were held in our sitting room so that we could lend our voices to the anthems. Yes, we had a piano, which along with the dining room suite constituted our most prized possessions. The piano was my old one from home, a wedding gift from Mom and Pop; the suite—black oak with a Welsh dresser—was a wedding gift from Mum and Dad. Our sitting room chairs were family cast-offs, and whereas the children each had a bed, our own sleeping was done on a mattress on the floor. This was an arrangement that horrified the midwife who arrived, none too early, to deliver our third baby; she demanded that it be somehow raised for her convenience and our obliging male neighbours brought in bricks and planks from the still-uncleared building site to make a platform for this purpose. I remember thankfully rolling back onto the newly lifted mattress and reaching for the gas and air just as Alan declared I didn't need that now, and I could have killed him had a weapon been handy.

Margaret Elizabeth Jane, named to please both grandmas, was our biggest and bounciest baby who rather surprised us by being a girl; I was convinced she would be a boy and in many ways as she grew up she resembled one, forever climbing trees. But for the time being she was just our latest precious child, duly baptized by John with fine godparents from the Crosdale family, and 25 Partridge Avenue was to be, we thought, our lasting home.

Or was it? Alan began to talk emigration again as he tussled with an ever-increasing workload and a never-increasing salary. The three doctors with whom he worked as the junior and least remunerated assistant were not inclined, after Suez, to expedite his promotion, and among them the four practitioners were looking after over 11,000 patients. This was just one of the ways the NHS erred, and Alan was one of many young doctors for whom the future seemed bleak indeed. Having held out in favour of remaining loyal to England, I finally capitulated the night he came home desperately ill with flu after fifteen hours continuous visiting of sick patients. I said we should explore the options available, just so long as we remained in the Commonwealth. This was enough to encourage him in his quest. In the next couple of months we looked at Australia and New Zealand—both too far away from Britain—and Canada, where one Ian Wood had advertised in the *BMJ* (*British Medical Journal*) for an assistant in rural Saskatchewan. He himself had but recently moved there from his former practice in Yorkshire—another disaffected young physician—and his letters were warm and informative. What is more, his young wife Barbara, herself also a physician though presently devoted to child rearing, wrote to me with all the advice another immigrant wife might need to have. We felt we had discovered friends, and thus the die was cast. The hard part lay ahead. What did we really know about Saskatchewan? A visit to Canadian Immigration offices in Liverpool helped not at all; the chap meeting our inquiries was himself from Montreal and knew nothing about the prairies, except that there were no roads and our children would have, he said, to go to school on horseback. Oh, and it would be hot in summer, and inimically cold in winter. Our home, heavily mortgaged, failed to sell, and we had to leave it in the hands of an attorney—a neighbour who had to sell his own house first.

But the worst thing of all was telling our parents of our decision. Mom and Pop demurred not at all, though I knew my mother felt it to be a mortal blow. My dear father said what I knew he would say: "My wench, I don't mind where you go in this world as long as I know you are all right." Dad, ever positive, said he would have done the same thing as a young man, and his son's future was likely to be much more secure in Canada. Mum remained tight lipped. But privately she phoned me to ask me to refuse to go abroad. She said what I knew to be true, that if I refused to go Alan would stay in England. We cried together as I explained why he had made this decision, and why I thought it right to go with him. Having now three children of my own, I understood her grief and could only promise that in three years we would come home again for a visit.

Alan said his final good-bye to the Wythenshaw practice in May and left for Rose Valley, Saskatchewan, that same month. I was left to sell the car (to raise money for our air tickets), sell up the furnishings (ditto), and generally wind up our affairs. Neighbours helped us to pack our personal effects, including wedding gifts of china (which suffered dismally on the journey). There were several parties and tearful farewells, and we finally walked across the tarmac at Manchester airport, a mother and three bairns, in July 1958.

The trials of the subsequent journey have often been told. It involved a three-stage piston- engined flight—Gander; Montreal; Saskatoon (plus an unscheduled stop-off for refueling in Thunder Bay)—and for me thirty-six hours of tending to those three bairns. Simon was trying hard to "look after Mommy," as he had been told to do, and dutifully sat still in airport lounges with Alison and teddy bear firmly in tow, listening anxiously to all the announcements. His reward was an Air Canada prize for his drawing of the airport in Gander. Alison climbed all over me at every opportunity demanding cuddles, Margi was fed at increasingly irregular intervals as my breast milk dwindled, and I had no alternative, nor could I find any, until an obliging fellow mother lent me a bottle. For much of the journey Margi obligingly slept in the provided overhead cot, but changing her (cloth) nappies (diapers) was a nightmare. As the hostess went through the spiel about routines to follow in the event of disaster I could think only of the insoluble problem: which babe would I save first?

I cannot remember sleeping at all during those hours of trial. I can remember the question of an indifferent stewardess, "Whoever heard of white coffee?" when I had responded "White, please" to her question about how I liked my coffee. I also remember her blithe announcement as we circledover Montreal that we should be arriving "momentarily." Where, I wondered, would we be takingoff for at once? Were we not to go through immigration procedures there? Indeed we were, and indeed we did, and what I remember most vividly of all is my first experience of the rudeness of French Canadian officials when they were dealing with the loathed English. Not for the only time, French Canadians scorned my fluent French and happily reduced me to tears.

Part III

New Canadians

S<small>IMON MUST HAVE</small> asked me at least a dozen times "When shall we see Daddy?" and after the nightmare of Montreal I confidently answered that it would be the next time the plane came down. Alas, the unscheduled landing in Fort William (Thunder Bay) made an unwitting liar of me, but how do you explain that to a four-year-old? I struggled on with more reading of *The Flopsy Bunnies*—the tenth time or so—to an uncomplaining two-year-old and persevered with persuading an unwilling six-month-old to take milk from the teat of an unfamiliar bottle, until finally, finally, the plane began its descent into the Saskatoon airport.

It was a bedraggled trio that made its way across the tarmac: I, with elephantine ankles, burdened by baby and Teddy and bags and blankets, while Simon and Alison each clung to either side of my skirt.

And there he was, my buoyant waiting Alan, wearing a white Stetson and standing beside the biggest car I had ever seen. At once the children were scooped up, hugged, and stashed into the back seat, where they obligingly fell asleep.

No such luck for me however. It was Pionera weekend in the city. There was no hotel room available. Nothing for it but to drive the 150 miles northeast to Rose Valley. The children slept sweetly on, and I longed to join them. But as we bumped along the 1958 gravel roads, there was so much that was new and strange to see. "Look! Look! Did you ever see such a sky!" "There are your first elevators!" "See the sunset on the slough!" "Those fields are full of wheat!" Finally "Look! Rape!" That one really made me sit up.

"Where?" But all there was to see was field upon field of glorious golden blooms. This was my first encounter with the strangely named canola blossom.

Three hours later we reached our destination, the municipal doctors' residence in the village of Rose Valley. This rambling old homestead had been seconded to us by the Wood family because they had only two children to our three, and they were, as we already knew from their letters—and Alan from first-hand experience—kindest of hosts and truest of friends. On the morrow I would meet them. Meantime … the landlord/owner of this old house, confidently expecting us to be staying the night in Saskatoon and arriving the following day, had taken out all the storm windows to repaint and every room was full of mosquitoes. These pesky creatures loved English blood.

Alan had minimally furnished the bedrooms, two upstairs for the children and one in the room off the (empty) sitting room for ourselves. This open-to-the-night-sky space was supplied with a borrowed "honeymoon" bed (sloping from each side into the middle) and also contained cupboards for luggage and the ever-to-be-ringing cranked telephone. Trekking back through sitting room and kitchen and past the porch door we came upon a bathroom with a chemical toilet in the corner and a claw-footed bath apparently hooked up to a water supply. Beaming, Alan assured me that we not only had running water to bathe in, but it was heated to boot. Triumphantly he turned the tap, and out streamed the brownest water I had ever seen. Hot—well, warm— indeed, but murky as the third witch's hell. It was then explained to me that this water was collected by a piping system from the roof, and thence channelled into a cistern in the basement. Certainly it was not for drinking (such water was delivered daily by horse and cart), but it was quite safe to bathe in. However, we should conserve it as much as possible. Thereupon he half-filled Margi's little bathtub, and each child was duly and perfunctorily washed. An evening ritual thus began; first Margi, then Alison, then Simon would be sat in the tub and sponged. I would then save their bath water to wash my feet before using it the next day to wash the kitchen floor—it would be put into as many uses as possible before finally being permitted to escape to water the veggies.

My questions about the state of the basement cistern would eventually be answered when a prowling cat fell into it one night. Hearing the caterwauling, Alan jumped in to save the animal, in pyjamas and bare feet, and thus encountered objects on the bottom of the tank, including a salamander. The tank was duly emptied and scraped out (ugh!) and the eaves unclogged so that the blessed rainwater and snow could now be less contaminated.

Meanwhile a dour Scot, Mr. Campbell, made his daily delivery of what he assured us was clean drinking water, pouring it into our container on the kitchen counter with only a few splashes. When questioned about the source of this water, he said it came from a local slough and was triple filtered—the filters he then showed Alan were made of chicken wire. Needless to say all water we drank, usually in the form of tea, was mightily boiled. The saved cat adopted us, as did our first Canadian dog, a black Lab named Tinker, and both slept in our porch for the three years we spent in Rose Valley.

Our first day as citizens of this fair village (which achieved official status as such when we brought its numbers up by five) was auspicious. I met for the first time our new extended family, Ian, Barbara, and their two sons Jim and Angus, whose home was just across the railroad tracks, along with Charlie and Alice Gavel, their next-door neighbours. Charlie was a Métis, as prairie descendants of Louis Riel were called, chairman of the hospital board, and immensely good company. Alice taught the first grade in the local school and would become Simon's first teacher.

That first summer was full of surprises. We took a weekend camping trip up to Waskesiu, north of Prince Albert, and closely encountered wildlife (a skunk) sniffing around our tent. We were advised by the RCMP that unlike in England camping was not permitted except at registered campsites. I found shopping for food quite bewildering because of different names (cornstarch instead of corn flour; cookies instead of biscuits; ketchup instead of tomato sauce). A steak was as big as the Sunday joint used to be. Margi was rapidly using up all her cloth nappies, and when I went in search of new ones at the local drugstore (used to be chemist), I was sent to the hardware store (shop), where I was shown some little glass bowls.

"Nappies?"

"Yup," replied Norbert Rustad, also our next-door neighbour, "fruit nappies. Not what you are wanting?" I regretfully, and with some mirth, explained the purpose to which I intended to put nappies. "Oh," he said, "you want diapers. Ask at the drugstore!" Chastened, I returned to find what I needed. Meanwhile Alan was happy as a king, his new hospital a kingdom, and Ian a brother monarch. We purchased furniture (hideous stuff but better than nowt), a complete living-room set from Eaton's catalogue, and a bedroom suite from a chap in Tisdale. The sun was hot and the sky huge, the countryside was full of lakes and sloughs and wild roses, and the children were bonny and blithe and good and gay. We took endless cine films of them to send home to our parents, and at Christmas there would be mutual ones taken with the Wood family, which would go the rounds from Brum to Stoke to Sheffield. Letters came regularly, all our folks being determinedly cheerful, and I replied in the same vein. But I was spending hours at the kitchen sink composing letters in my head that I would never send.

The simple truth was that I was desperately homesick those first few weeks. Barbara was my great comfort. She knew what I was feeling, and encouraged me to talk about it over endless cups of tea or "cawffee" (with cream, Canadian "white") while our children played together in the yard (garden). Before long we had become sisters, each family being now an extended family of the other one, and every second month or so Babs and I escaped to the big city of Saskatoon for a shopping spree together. We jointly staffed the Ladies' Hospital Aid and visited new native mothers—usually at fifteen or so—in the hospital where our husbands ran such a busy practice.

But still I missed my English home. Then came an evening when, on entering a schoolroom for a community meeting, I exclaimed about the smell of the chalk. Like the smell of greasepaint, so evocative for me. The following morning the principal of the high school stood on my doorstep asking if I would consider teaching. Like right away. It was a time when secondary teachers were in very short supply.

Well, there being such an amplitude of housekeeper-nannies available, I quickly agreed. Soon I was teaching (social studies, composition, and home ec) in grades eleven and twelve. By the next year I had proved competent enough to be offered literature in place of the home ec and become deeply enmeshed in extracurricular activities such as a girls' choir and a drama group. By my second year I had mounted a production of *Toad of Toad Hall*. This was followed by "The Gulling of Malvolio" (scenes from *Twelfth Night*), which won the high school drama festival, and a truncated version of Gilbert and Sullivan's *The Mikado*, which toured the province and appeared on CBC radio. Evidently my life had now become so full of rewarding activities that I no longer gave myself up to mooning about the home I had left behind. Ironically, the literature texts I was now teaching were largely English, particularly Shakespeare and the Romantic poets, so I had ample opportunity to revel in language quite unfamiliar to my lovable students, who were mostly of farming stock and of Ukrainian or Scandinavian heritage. What did they know of skylarks or nightingales? I'm sad to say I spent some teaching time on enlightening them about the English birds and the English spring, and they put up with such gratuitous instruction because they so enjoyed my accent. They would chant, "Say it again, Mrs. Clews!" when I used a word such as "water."

That first winter was horrendously cold, but the trees loaded with hoarfrost under a brilliantly sunny sky were beautiful indeed, and soon I was writing rapturous letters home about the billowing northern lights, and the unstinting hospitality of my friendly new neighbours. Though snow abounded, deep and soft, it was too cold for it to be wet, and little rotund Margi would come in after an hour of frolicking with her siblings, or snowballing Jim and Angus, her cheeks as red as her enveloping snowsuit. She would then shake herself as vigorously as Tinker did, and emerge from her crimson padding dry and warm. By now, at a year old, she was prattling away and asking to go to "Sassakoonin" with "Auntie Barbar" at regular intervals. Meanwhile her older brother and sister looked after her well. They also performed an operation on the beloved Teddy to see (Simon's enquiring mind) where the "Rock-a-Bye Baby" song came from when his tummy was pressed. Alas, he never sang again.

But I skip too far ahead. Mutual retirement was nearly thirty years ahead of us. Meantime I had to finish out my last term at Rose Valley High School and prepare for the family trip to "the old country," as old-timers called their native lands. I became pregnant again, and thereby hangs an oft-told tale I will spare Mandy. By the time we flew back across the Atlantic, she was making her presence felt and giving us another Canadian to introduce to our parents. For this, they quickly saw, was what we had all become, and there was no likelihood of our ever coming back to them for good. We therefore exchanged promises; we would return every four or five years for visits home, and they would come to see us in Saskatchewan as soon as could be arranged.

Our lovely new home in Kerrobert was most welcoming. It was directly across the street from the new Kerrobert/Luseland Hospital, so I didn't have far to go when our new baby's birth was imminent and Tom O'Halloran, Alan's new Irish partner, barely arrived in time to deliver her. He was delighted when we decided to name her for his lovely wife, Madeleine, herself the mother of five.

The following year my parents, Mom and Pop, were true to their word. My dear father, who had told me when we emigrated that he didn't care where in the world I lived so long as he knew I was well and happy, and who had never before left his hometown for more than a short bus ride, actually boarded a plane and flew to the other side of the world. We took them both on a camping trip to Banff, where he was thrilled to be able to watch hummingbirds in the gardens of the Banff Springs Hotel. He and Mom enjoyed visiting with the locals in Kerrobert and their three weeks' visit quickly passed. I was never to see him again.

Our six years in Kerrobert went by very quickly. I became the only teacher of senior English in the local high school, and adjudicator for high school festivals throughout the province. At eleven Simon became so frustrated by having to wait for other class members to master long division he refused to go back to school, and to my immense regret he became a boarder at St. John's-Ravenscourt in Winnipeg. His sisters adapted more readily. These were also the years of our deepest losses. In November of 1962 Alan's mother, Lily of beloved memory, died of ovarian cancer. When Alan rushed to visit her a month earlier, she was beyond communicating with him and he returned to us traumatized by the knowledge that had she been in Canada she would probably have been treated more effectively. In fact I recall his having received a letter from his father Walter describing her symptoms, and saying at once on reading it through, "But this is a carcinoma." In fact it was his immediate letter to Lily's GP that finally alerted that overworked physician to the possible diagnosis, which was then made too late.

The following summer Dad came over for the visit they had intended to make together, and we all drove to the west coast with tents and trailer (caravan). Like us, Dad was at once enchanted by the British ambiance and diversity we encountered on Vancouver Island. We travelled the narrow logging road through Alberni to Long Beach, and on our way back through Cathedral Grove and Englishman's River we discovered blackberries. Joy! We crammed fistfuls into the men's hats, which would never be the same again, and the children's sand buckets, not considering what we could possibly do with them on a camp stove in a campsite. Truly a surfeit of berries. When he flew home again, Dad said that one day he would return to stay in this paradise, and we knew he meant it. What none of us could know were the changes that still lay ahead for all of us.

It was in the cold wet winter of 1964—wet cold, not at all like the dry cold of Saskatchewan—that my father succumbed to pneumonia. He had been suffering from silicosis for as long as I could remember, and given his history it is not surprising. As the eldest son of his family he left school at eleven to become the breadwinner for his mother and six siblings, and toiled as an iron moulder in the factory of Lowe and Brookes in Blackheath. For six years, between the ages of five and eleven, it was my job to take him his lunch in an oilcloth bag—doorstep sandwiches and a bottle of cold tea—and for me the entrance to the yard where he worked was the nearest I ever came to the hell of Catholic tradition. The furnace fires, visible as soon as the gate clanged shut behind me, were mightily flaring and belching forth acrid smoke. In the gloom of the factory floor I would see Pop staggering as he carried heavy trays of molten iron from the furnace to his filthy workspace, or jumping up and down on the core tray. He would motion me to sit one of the upturned buckets that served him as seat and table, but I could never get out of that hell fast enough. Blackheath was the centre of the Black Country from the time of the Industrial Revolution up until postwar cleanups closed so many factories and clean community air became the issue of the day. But by this time it was too late for my father, and though his new work assembling electrical appliances was relatively benign, he continued to suffer from the dreadful cough I remember keeping him—and Mom and me—awake at night. Well, the news of his death came to Kerrobert with the severest of snowstorms, and my mother quickly followed. She left her home and our dog in the care of her closest sister, Pem, to whom she gave no promised time of return. It was to be a winter of mourning and healing for both of us. Of course, spring inevitably followed, and as her spirits lifted, Mom decided it was time to return to the home she no longer wished to live in. Arrangements were made to sell 4 Walton Avenue to Pem, and Mom began a determined hunt for a new home, preferably a place in the country with a large garden. Who better to drive her on weekend forays around Worcestershire than Alan's father?

What happened next was totally unexpected. They found a home in which Walter declared they should henceforth live together, so that soon they were man and wife, and he was my "double-dad." It all made perfect sense. After all, they had a ready-made family in common, and as Alan was quick to point out, he and I closely resembled his father and my mother respectively, and we were good enough together, so why did I find the idea of their union so difficult?

I could only repeat that to me my mother was exclusively my father's wife. As usual, it took only a little time for me to accept that she could indeed become attuned to a very different partner; two of her great strengths were flexibility and ready compliance. Simon was troubled, and in his usual way asked a series of questions days apart. First he wanted to know if we—that is, Alan and I—would now be brother and sister. Next he asked if we could now go on being married to one another. His final question was, "If Grandma and Granddad have a baby, what will it be to me?" I was thus enabled to complete his birds and bees education by explaining that Grandma was now too old to be having any more babies. And that was finally that. Soon we were off on a plane to see them in their new home in Bourneheath, Worcestershire, where Double-Dad was already talking about how they might themselves emigrate on his retirement in a few years time.

Once back in Kerrobert, however, I was becoming restless. Being cast in a couple of summer players' productions in Saskatoon, first as Nancy in *Oliver* and next as Guinevere in *Camelot,* whetted my appetite for living in that beautiful city, and teaching in a high school was not the way I wanted to spend the rest of my life. It seemed the time had come for another move, this time to a city in which I could enrol at a fine university and complete the master's degree I had begun in Birmingham fifteen years earlier. The decision was made, many tearful farewells were expressed, a home was found in the suburbs near good schools, Alan joined Dr. Joseph Brook in family practice, and I took up a teaching appointment in the city high school of Mount Royal. From this point on I was to coedit the English teachers' magazine, *Skylark*, and so begin a new avocation as a writer of several essays, poems, and plays. Thus confirmed in what seemed to be a new pathway in my professional career, I approached the English Department at the University of Saskatchewan in Saskatoon.

I would like, please, I said, to finish my thesis on Blake and thus complete my master's degree. The advisor looked at me in surprise. Did I not know there were stringent requirements for entry into graduate school? Where were my transcripts?

My own surprise was considerable. Typically British, I scorned the mere idea of "transcripts." They had been unheard of at the University of Birmingham, where a degree was classified (First, 2A, 2B, 3, or Pass) and one needed at least a 2A to enter graduate school. I had received a double first. But there were no numbers attached, and the subject areas, especially in poetry, were at least fifteen years out of date. I had no American or Canadian literature studies, both essential for the U of S. No, the only way to prove my eligibility was by taking a make-up year in literature, and attaining an 80 percent average in five subjects: the two essential ones plus modern American poetry, modern English poetry, and a period of my choice by century. I chose the eighteenth century and gritted my teeth. I'd show them.

The next year was a tough one. I taught mornings at City Park High School, attended university classes afternoons and evenings, all the time looking after the family. A housekeeper with her own little girl babysat Mandy, who by next year would be in grade one. By June I had comfortably passed the 80 percent average and earned a teaching fellowship, and I was on the academic ladder. No more high school teaching, and a new MA subject in Virginia Woolf, there being no Blake scholar, nor indeed any theologian, in sight. As a teaching fellow I had several first-year classes to instruct and scholarship money with which to finance three years of grad studies. I also had a new mentor in Keith Johnstone, of Bloomsbury Group fame, whom I soon learned to love and esteem highly.

Meanwhile I continued to edit professional journals and to write the odd poem as well as several plays for children, including a couple of British-type pantomimes in which my talented daughters starred. For a class in the Modern Novel, I wrote a piece based on my experience of Gran's death. It shows me fictionalized as "Hilda," and rearranges the time frame to include reference to my Yorkshire teaching experience (I was actually nineteen and at university when the described bedside vigils took place). I also changed my physical appearance to become the tall and willowy creature I had always wished to be, but in all other regards this story is based on truth. I now find this writing interesting, in retrospective, as evidence of my contention that the boundaries between so-called "truth" and "fiction" are always and inevitably arbitrary. (Also the autobiographical novel I intended to write was never finished, though scraps of it survive among my papers.)

From '68 to '74 were education years for the entire family. Alan gained his fellowship in the college of Family Medicine and further qualifications in addictions and aboriginal health. Margi was offered special education on entering grade five, as later was Mandy also, and they both loved school. Alison wrongly thought herself the dummy of the family, but it was an accident of timing alone that accounted for her being too old, once we moved to the city, to enter the academic special stream provided by the Saskatoon School Board, and she easily achieved university entrance in her graduation year at the excellent Aden Bowman Collegiate, where Margi was to follow her. Simon meanwhile continued his colourful life as a boarder at SJ-R, arriving home to startle us with his new hairstyles at holiday time, and continuing his vigilance as big brother by screening the various boyfriends who had begun to seek out his sisters. He decided on graduation to take a degree at Queen's University in Kingston, Ontario, and later followed the rest of us out west.

The rest of us by now included the grandparents, who emigrated to live in sunny Sidney in 1966, beginning a pattern of visits we were to follow for the next eight years. They would usually come to us for a Saskatchewan Christmas, commonly shared with the Woods, and we would spend our summer vacation on a camping trip to the west coast where we would stay with them in Sidney as long as we could. The only time we tried travelling by car to Sidney for Christmas we found the journey harrowing—snowstorms and cancelled ferries and poor little Mandy suffering from car sickness. It became the occasion for one of our family car songs, of which there were many over the years:

> We six Clews from Saskatoon are
> Bearing gifts we travel by car
> Field and fountain, moor and mountain
> To get to Victoria
> O car of wonder, car of might
> Car piled high with Clewses so bright
> Westward leading, still proceeding
> Drive us to our grandma's tonight

(Remember also "Doughnuts taste good with peanut butter"?)

It was not education alone, however, that filled the Saskatoon years with pleasurable activity. There was much theatre for all of us, severally and together. Alan and I scored a great success in *My Fair Lady* as Higgins and Eliza, and we appeared together not only in pantomimes but also in *Fiddler on the Roof, Brigadoon*, and *The Music Man* (for which I gained notoriety, as well as incurring permanent spinal damage, by falling off the stage backward into the orchestra pit. "Nice of you," said the conductor Bob Horden, never missing a beat, "to drop in.") Alan and I both won awards for acting, and I also won several for directing, in Theatre Saskatchewan and Theatre Canada. With our close friends Rosemary and Dennis Hunt we appeared in the play that represented the prairie-provinces at the last of the national theatre festivals in St. John's Newfoundland.

At home I taught drama classes for Saskatoon's Theatre for Children and also at the penitentiary in Prince Albert, where I had taken both my production of John Bowen's *The Fall and Redemption of Man* (with Mandy—the youngest ever guest of that establishment—as a lamb) and a play I was currently directing for Gateway Theatre. This last was the aptly named *The Night Thoreau Spent in Jail* by Lawrence and Lee, and Gateway supported the endeavour by offering weekend workshops in acting to the interested inmates and enabling them to put on their own winning play at the Saskatoon Theatre Festival in 1973.

Margi and Mandy went on from strength to strength in the local academic programmes and in their music, while Alison discovered boys. Or rather they discovered her. I defended my master's thesis the day the faculty club burned down and went on to complete all course work for a PhD, pursuing an idea of my own about the development of the novel. Keith heartily approved and all signals were set fair. With Simon and Alison both on the brink of finding their own places to live, we decided to move to a smaller home in the prestigious university area and bought 1014 University Drive, former home of my dear eighteenth-century professor Peter Millard, in the fall of '73. It was handy for both me and Alison, now registered in the College of Education for her freshman year, to cross College Drive from our front door on foot.

Then it was that very different scenes began to unfold, because our lovely eighteen-year-old decided to marry her high school sweetheart the following year, and suddenly we found ourselves arranging a summer wedding. Mom and Dad and the Woods were all invited, and I began frantic dressmaking for bride and bridesmaids. Meanwhile, Mom found herself troubled by what appeared to be a recurrence of her earlier breast cancer and we came to the hasty decision that we would move out west soon after the wedding. The day after, in fact, for me and the children, and October for Alan, who needed two months to wind up his practice with Joe Brook.

We duly set off on what turned out to be a calamitous journey, with an unlooked-for sojourn in Calgary while my poor old Toyota received a new transmission. Then the two younger girls and I camped out in the new house we had found on Shorncliffe Road in the Saanich area of Victoria, while I took a course at the University of Victoria in preparation for teaching there a few weeks later. In retrospect, the summer of '74 was an altogether tumultuous time, providing turning points for everyone. By the time Alan joined us, I was embarked on a program of teaching graduate students how to teach English. This would change in 1978, when my finally granted PhD permitted me to move from the Department of Education to the Department of English, where I began twelve further years of sessional appointments for which I was underpaid, but, as time went on, offered whatever privileges were possible to an untenured scholar who had suffered first from sexism, and more recently from ageism. I directed musical shows for the university as well as teaching as far afield as Nanaimo, Cranbrook, and even Boca Raton. I also enjoyed summers and one whole year as a visiting professor at the U of S, which enabled me to spend time with Margi's little family. Alison's Sarah, and her sisters Rachel and Katherine, had by now settled into west coast living, as had Simon and family, and Madeleine's wedding was on the horizon. Alan meantime joined in family practice with Bill Falk and Andy Swan. He happily embarked on his crusade against drug and alcohol dependency with the Life Enrichment Society, which he co-founded with Charles Aharan, and at which he worked, along with Martin Spray, for the next eighteen years. Meanwhile, no sooner had my mother achieved her goal of having her daughter close at hand than she became symptom free, and entertained us weekly at her Sidney home.

West Coasters

THE TURNING POINT in our Victorian experience came in 1977, when we exchanged our trim little home on Shorncliffe for a rambling older home in Cordova Bay, perched on a hill above Sayward Beach.

The house at 5345 Parker Avenue was to be our beloved family home for the next twelve years. In its beach-top garden three grandchildren were baptized and, in 1986, our youngest daughter was married. We built there a "granny flat" for Mom and Double-Dad, though alas he did not survive the move from Sidney to his new home long enough to benefit from it. He died in our ocean-view library watching and listening to the sea later in that same year of 1982, just after he heard of the birth of his firstborn great-grandson, Justin, who, as Simon's son, carried on the family surname. Mom was able to enjoy her spanking new kitchen and living quarters, however; she walked through the laundry to take her evening meal with us and mostly prepared her own lunches. I fell into a routine of providing a breakfast tray for her in bed before I set off on my teaching day, and taking her shopping every Tuesday afternoon, when I had no classes. She particularly loved going to the Woodward's "$1.49 day" and kept me thus supplied with soap and Scotch tape and other sundries. We now encouraged and appreciated visits from family in England and old friends in Canada and the States, having at last plenty of room for them to stay with us. Our sequential boats—Circe and Venus and Gaia—we kept moored in our own bay below the house, and as we spent several summer holidays sailing among the Gulf Islands we were able to find the ideal spot on Salt Spring where we would build our retirement home. We also persuaded Ian and Barbara Wood to buy property alongside what we had chosen as the site. And in 1986 Alan was among the first to circumnavigate Vancouver Island, which he did with some help from Simon. This is commemorated in a plaque with the title "The Island Odyssey," which names him as participant in this first-ever circumnavigation by private crafts.

Mom meanwhile sallied forth to Britain and her surviving sisters there several times as a second-time-around widow, and it was while accompanying her home again at the end of my own summer visit in 1987 that I found myself dealing with the emergency of a sudden heart attack in the mid-Atlantic, which took her straight to hospital in Vancouver. Thereafter she persevered with a pacemaker and accepted her reduced mobility. Though she participated gladly in our plans to re locate to Salt Spring Island, choosing paint and wallpaper for the suite we were building for her there, she succumbed to heart failure a mere two months before we finally made the move in 1989. This self-contained annex to our new home became "G. G.'s place," and as such was used by the family and many visitors over the next ten years.

A Smaller Island

W E SPENT ALMOST twenty years on Salt Spring Island, the longest we have ever sojourned in Canada. Of these years, half were spent on Reginald Hill, alongside Fulford Harbour, in the house we had designed to accommodate ourselves and G. G. (Mom). This was just down the hill from Ian and Barbara's place. They moved into retirement there the same time that we did. Our other cherished neighbour was Robert Bateman, for whom Alan often supplied birds, and with whom—along with his gifted wife Birgit—we soon became good friends. There were three separate beaches on our property, which Alan ingeniously reconfigured to make into eight discrete areas—one each for our grandchildren, who became the only Canadian progeny to have beaches named for them individually. On an early summer visit of the Saskatchewan thread, we put up signs at the ferry dock: "This way to Sam's beach and Em's beach."

There was plenty of room in this cherished home for many Christmas and summer reunions, with visits from our many scattered friends. There was also plenty for newly retired professionals to be doing on the island. Alan fast became a valued trailblazer and kayaker, while I channelled my energies into serving on the board of the newly designed (but not yet built) ArtSpring and teaching adult classes in literature.

We both sang in several choirs, acted and/or directed plays, and supported the local churches as well as the community at large by our work as peer counsellors, senior services volunteers, and active members of hospice. In fact we found ourselves busy in many unanticipated ways, so that gradually the care of house and garden and the frequency of trips into Ganges caused us to wonder if we should not perhaps move to a smaller and more central home. The seal was set on this by a road accident in which I disastrously swerved to avoid a small furry animal and redamaged my already twisted spine. Remember *The Music Man*?

My latest accident led not only to hospitalization, but also to an exacerbation of my already widespread osteoarthritis to a degree that severely limited my mobility. Thus it was we found ourselves seeking a one-level home closer to Ganges and rejoiced when we came upon one next door to two of our favourite people, Lorne Bunyan, former police chief, and his wife Shirley, the organist/choir mistress of the United Church. Here we entered our second phase as Salt Springers while retaining earlier friendships and clubs such as Trail and Nature for Alan and the precious Book Club for me. Here also we found our disaffection with the language and political policies of the United Church of Canada persuading us to revert to an earlier loyalty to the Anglican Church and in it we were soon happily at home. All Saints' Church became the venue for Ian's memorial when he died in November 2007. This was also the church that accommodated my last writing/directing venture on the island, *Boney and the Billy Ruffians*, and accepted me as a worker in the kitchen for its various delectable public meals. The home on Canvasback was indeed less commodious than its predecessor, but upstairs there were two extra sleeping spaces and an extra bathroom as well as Alan's study, so we were still able to house the family members who occasionally visited. In 2003, memorably, we also filled several local B&Bs with the overflow of those who came to celebrate our golden wedding anniversary; Alison and Margi will remember a story about the consequences of one such accommodation.

But time was taking its toll in terms of health and endurance. When I found the stresses of being so far from my children, with water and increasingly costly ferry fares between us, too much to bear, we agreed to move back to Victoria—the larger island—again. In December 2007 we found the condominium in which we were to spend a couple of years, finding there new groups and activities to divert us.

The year 2009 marked our eightieth birthdays, and with this in mind we arranged a trip for the entire family—children, grandchildren, and their significant others—to Maui for a week of family celebrations. This proved to be a heavenly and unforgettable occasion, as commemorated in the Maui song written by Mandy.

Maui 09 Anthem

And now, as I sit here writing this last section, it seems we have finally come to rest at Amica House on Douglas here in Victoria, where our every need is being met, and where the greatest event of our recent lives has been the birth, to Sarah and her Geoff, of our first great-grandchild, Colin Geoffrey Wilson, or Cole. More good things are to come. Alison's youngest, Katie, is betrothed to her Dave, while her middle daughter, our sweet Rachel, is also expecting her first child—a girl already named Ryan—in May. And so it goes on, the weaving of new tapestries by hands other than mine.

Finally, there are those who will not be able to read this, but whose preciousness merits mention before I close. All our lives we have cherished cats and dogs, from Alan's boyhood companion, Rack, and my girlhood pets, Nell and Jazz, to the series we have shared with the children. Many cats have favoured us with their patronage, from the homeless Fishie that Alan rescued from the cistern in Rose Valley through PG (Prince Gautama) and Tinkabel to Alison's Panther and Sarah's George and Delilah. And innumerable strays—blessed comfort-givers all. Among our canine friends let us not forget Rose Valley's Tinker; Kerrobert's Charlie (so much a member of the family that among Kerrobert's citizens he rejoiced in the full name of Charlie Clews), who habitually waited for me outside the school, moving from window to window to watch me in the classrooms, and who on Sundays (how did he know the day?) attended us in the church porch. Then in Saskatoon there was Sirius, who came out west with us. He it was accompanied us on our annual trips from Saskatoon to Sidney, on one occasion getting himself left behind in Mitchell, Montana, at a business loop that contained only an hotel and a gas station. When we discovered he was missing and retraced our journey, there he patiently sat beside the solitary gas pump.

On Salt Spring there was the special long-haired dachsie, Clancy ("He's really quite a dog/ Clancy, he smells like wet warthog/Clancy, he's not so fancy/he cannot dance/he can't even climb stairs—thanks for the lyrics, Shel!), who was followed by our darling bichon frise, Frosty, of sailing expertise. Finally came the only female among them, little malti-poo, Perky, who is still, praise be, adoringly with us.

This is Perky "in her favourite place"

In addition there have been many adopted and fostered pets such as Tess, Jess, Prue, Bear, Pretzel, Torque, Zoe, and Gidget—only my failing memory forces me to close the list and say: "Let us now praise famous dogs, canine partners who adored us. All these were honoured in their generation and were the glory of their time." All denizens of our shining places and, if Lord Dunsany is to be believed, reincarnations there. And so the time has come to turn over the tapestry and discover the design in this lifetime's work.

And so, again, in our end is our begining.

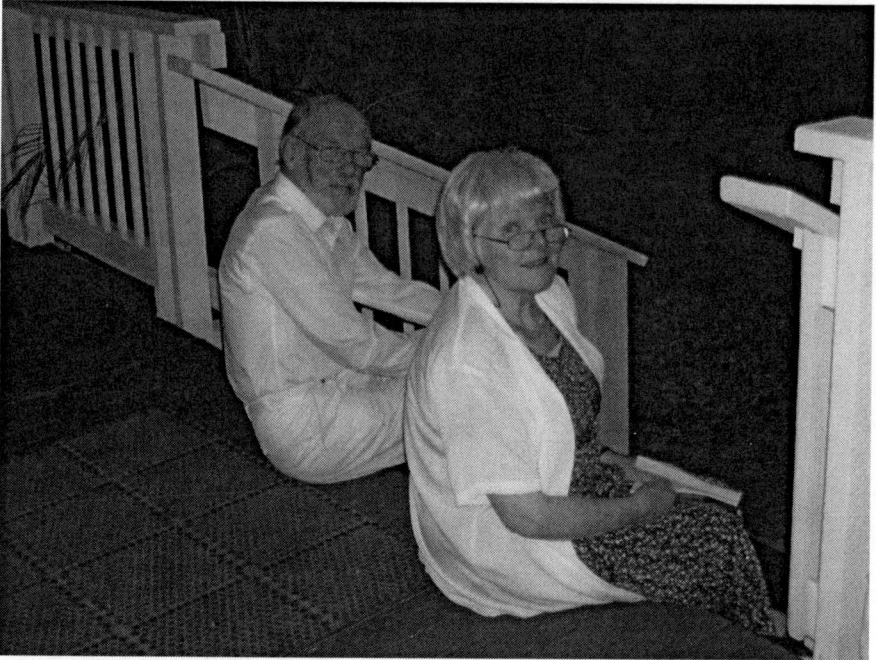

After 58 years – were there ever two of us?

CPSIA information can be obtained at www.ICGtesting.com
Printed in the USA
237257LV00002B/10/P